A SHAPE IN THE NET

A Shape in the Net

FERGUS CHADWICK

PETERLOO POETS

First published in 1993
by Peterloo Poets
2 Kelly Gardens, Calstock, Cornwall PL18 9SA, U.K.

© 1993 by Fergus Chadwick

All rights reserved. No part of this publication may be reproduced, stored in a retrieval system, or transmitted, in any form or by any means, electronic, mechanical, photocopying, recording or otherwise without the prior permission in writing of the publisher.

A catalogue record for this book is available from the British Library

ISBN 1-871471-30-3

Printed in Great Britain by
Latimer Trend & Company Ltd, Plymouth

ACKNOWLEDGEMENTS Some of the poems in this collection have appeared in the following magazines: *Agenda, Encounter, Orbis, Chapman, Outposts* and *Weyfarers*, and have been broadcast on 'Poetry Now' (BBC Radio 4).

Supported by
Cornwall County Council

INVESTMENT SOUTH WEST ARTS

Contents

page
- 9   U.X.B.
- 10 Great War Style
- 11 Aerial Photos, Reconnaissance
- 12 Chameleon
- 13 Common Blues
- 14 Mouse Interview
- 15 The Wasp
- 16 The Garden Ambush
- 18 Spider Circus
- 19 Broadcasting on Oak
- 20 February Bird
- 21 The Crow
- 23 The Courting of the Peacock
- 24 Girl on an Outing
- 25 After You've Gone
- 26 Pegasus
- 27 Taking a Message
- 28 Nearly Caught
- 29 To Change by Eating
- 30 Sir Orfeo
- 31 The Emperor's Rose-Petal Dig
- 32 Kennedy's Revised Latin Primer
- 33 Entertaining Caesar
- 35 Rue Point
- 36 Cold Snap
- 37 Anniversaries
- 38 Tulip Folio
- 39 Painting in the Rain
- 40 Glass
- 41 Ariel
- 42 Portrait of a Pear
- 43 Damsons
- 44 English Discovery
- 45 West Green Garden
- 46 Night of Stars

47 Sharp, Bright, Dark
48 The Kaleidoscope
49 The Argument from Forgotten Corners
50 All Vagrom Men
51 Soup Kitchen
52 Hunter Gatherer
53 Paris: Winter Night
54 Apparitions
55 The Sower
56 The Asylum at St. Rémy
57 The Dark Side of the Moon
58 Baudelaire's Second Lecture
60 Kafka in the Cinema

U.X.B.

A bomber's moon they call it.
Searchlights, dimmed by distance,
roll round chimney-pots and trees,
developing their negatives of snow.

Then the sirens by Duchamp start,
surreal evensong, whose split
harmonic wail brings on the echelons
of swollen labouring metal birds.

Death in an airman's uniform
with mittened hands and leather head,
one eye to a hair-cross gauge,
blue underwings over-shot by beams.

A warden, in a helmet shiny
as a toffee-apple in the flames,
carries a pale child over and over
with smeary face from the debris.

The sister, whom your mother lay upon
to shield, peeps at the foot of her bed,
listening, as the throbbing planes fade,
to the tinkle of ambulance bells.

Swinging on its ashen drogue, one ton
of patient enmity falls unobserved,
so harsh that even after forty years
it hates all those who touch it.

Great War Style

Picasso recognised his Cubist style
on army trucks. Their scaly hides
were daubed with cheapo masterpieces;
Cézanne woods, harlequin diamonds,
or cannons with chocolate sauce on top.

Men hid in dummy trees to spy
like oracles inside a sacred stag;
but trees with windows,
trees with imitation bark,
with leaves of cloth,
and steps that led inside.

Field guns poked from nets of scrim,
decreasingly opaque towards the edge,
as if posed for a Vorticist picture.

Ships, dazzle-painted
with Les Demoiselles d'Avignon
—meat-cleaver profiles,
origami limbs folded to darts—
altered their size, shape, and course,
to hoodwink the periscope eye.

And these: were these automata?
Men hanging on the wire
as dummy substitutes for death.

Aerial Photos, Reconnaissance

They sweat under a one-eyed giant,
a Cyclopean magnifying-glass.
Hours long their ordeal
in some enemy office,
where experts hunch in green inquisition.
Our structures might sing;
an aerodrome, an ammo-dump, a factory,
emerge into focus from 'hedge' or 'lane'
like clues solved in a crossword.
Or the pictures seem just countryside,
as bland as any patchwork quilt,
remote as counterpanes mapped
out of sight by Messerschmidt.

Back home our Air Ministry men
build entire ghost landscapes.
Fake hills on lattices of steel,
grass netting they can walk across,
sham trees of wire in gauzy coils.
And next to them, a sail-cloth house
with windows painted on.
And underneath all this, buildings,
roads, mysterious stacks of boxes,
tins, anonymous supplies.

Aircraft emerge like insects
from their larval form,
their drab-and-green cloaked wings
clustered with bombs.

The fake walls part.
Mosquitoes drone into the night.

Chameleon

'Picasso said once that he who created a thing is forced to make it ugly. In the effort to create the intensity and the struggle to create this intensity, the result always produces a certain ugliness, those who follow can make of this thing a beautiful thing because they know what they are doing, the thing having already been invented, but the inventor because he does not know what he is going to invent inevitably the thing he makes must have its ugliness.'
Gertrude Stein, *Picasso*, 1938.

Snake in the grass
wolf in sheep's clothing
chameleon colours, we say.

This leather purse
on bendy-toy legs
knows all the vanitory arts.

It needs rose tints,
beige blusher, green foundation,
to match the living wall,

To hide a face
bursting with eyes
remote-controlled like videos.

To blend with fruits
and leaves, the better to zap
flies with its shillelagh tongue.

A painter's apprentice
would end up like this, bewitched;
a living grinder of colours,

Doomed to be the Spiritual Form
of a tyrant, despite his shenanigans
with the Impressionist palette.

Common Blues

'The vivid blue on the wings of the males is not a true colour at all, that is, it is not pigment. The blue that you see is refracted light as it strikes the thousands of minute scales, fixed like slates on a roof, to the upper surface of the butterfly's wings.'
L. Hugh Newman, *Linger and Look* p. 35.

On their wings
rise constellated circles,
silver-dark
as the eyes seen in birches,
chased finely
in blue metallurgy, art
of powders
in a winter chrysalis.
Yes, courtship
and flattery, up and down,
back and forth,
they stitch the bright forest gap
with speedwell
blue, their underwings velours
in the eyes
of one leaning dazzled still
with sun scent
of resin and dry heather,
one elbow
scored, one hand out to prevent
the squiggly
bushes tearing their blue silk,
their fringed hairs.

Mouse Interview

The grey pavement wriggles underfoot
and produces a creature,
tailed, furred, a thumb's-joint in length.
Cowed, but trustfully trembling,
it potholes down my clenched fist;
and submits its head to be stroked
by one beam-engine finger.
For my foot would have crushed it
where joggers' shoes smash the path.

He sits facing me, his high legs
dragging a ball-and-chain of fear.
He is an ambassador;
his fine claws are Lilliputian swords.
What language do we speak,
eye to eye; his, two mustard seeds?
There is no interpreter: beauty
alone says praise him, release him
from your giant pulpit of fingers.

He treads the iron gate,
and vanishes in woods of flower-stalks.

The Wasp

I saw his shadow first, drawn on the net.
All night long, while I slept,
he hooked his way up, up the glass ladder.
With infinite cold caution
in his stiffened limbs
he climbed above the rising condensation.

Forgotten, his ambitious murders,
or that he swaggered in striped stockings.
He took refuge the first chilly dusk,
and crawled this white window-sill
from one end to the other
like a racked prisoner in a cell.

But, finally, he reached the bright beam.
Now I saw him upright, prone in the dazzle,
his horned vizard face pressed to the sun,
as if *there* hung the mislaid vespiary,
the centre that kisses purpose,
that warms and tickles joints.

But the glass intervened:
keeping (and yet protecting) from the air
that roved with a warrant
and cold leg-irons for this Spaniard.
I opened to let him pass the ledge
of shadow, where he fumbled and fell.

The Garden Ambush

I watched the eight arms move into play,
    flexing the web,
leisurely wrapping a buzzing prey
    with surgeon's thread.

That morning in late summer it was
    hard not to feel
disgust at the number of shining
    wheels hanging there,

Each with its pot-bellied bag of pus
    springing the trap
when insects with wings shook frantically
    in sticky wires.

The invisible net sometimes touched
    my hand with silk,
or, worse, my face watching between flowers
    some other key.

The glistening jaws administered shock
    as well as pure
poison, like the old executions
    full of knowledge,

Where first your breath was choked out by rope,
    then the knife, then
the axe, then headless trunks stuck like these
    in a high place.

And here typically one admires the
    bright mechanics,
acquired so arduously one presumes
    evolution

Itself too short to yield the clue how
> such low-brows could
possibly plan these trampolines spun
> out of themselves.

They moved with hangman's immunity
> on the scaffold,
and I saw a rotten black parcel
> being sucked for food.

And that one I watched ignored me while
> its mandibles
went on picking over the dish. To
> make it let go

Seemed then the one feeble protest that
> morality
could advance in mitigation of
> guile and slaughter.

Loth to touch it I blew a quick breath,
> and it dropped in
the bushes with a pat, unable
> to keep tight hold.

But in my mind that body often
> steeplejacks a
line, hauling its satin hunchback up
> to feed again.

Spider Circus

She starts the performance, rain permitting;
for it is a jealous god
that all night drenches the herb-garden's
feathery plumes.
You and I don't hear it, perhaps,
but her silk handling
sounds like a hyacinth shoot
that squeaks as it extrudes.

Her green-room is so well concealed,
so perfectly obscure,
so without diplomatic reach,
that next-door's rose is another universe;
across the fence, unthinkably far.
Yet, the spotlight (sun obliging)
picks out her two millimetres,
freeing the brown-gold jacket,
two arms in a tiny drop of rain.
A tightrope
bends across a green canyon.
Down
on a line of herself,
not to any net, not to any
applausive murmur cresting like surf,
(as a jerk-stop saves her fall)
she plumbs an emerald darkness.
Her hair's-breadth attachments
knot and weave
an invisible, lethal trapeze.
No audience,
save you and I perhaps; evoked,
like Scots Bruce, by the spider's art;
admirers of persistent skill.
To do counts as praise.

Broadcasting on Oak

A jay screams—raucously ungreased—
a courtier goosed for a laugh.
Its screech is like a moggy's howl
of interrupted lust
in flower-beds drenched with shadow;
an irritant
like a torn fingernail on wool.
I see a young one in the morning
fly green corridors,
a puckfist bird; an oak-monitor
with sparky brocade waistcoat
flash as turquoise static;
with a punk crest on top
and a pink jammy-bastard bib.
Any acorn free of galls
that beak deftly nicks,
and trenches into soil
whose lid crackles with brown oak.
Scattered with earth,
the seed in its pine box
is shaped like an ancient microphone.

February Bird

Ballet has copied the thrush,
that old-fashioned lyrist of tat.
Entrechats, toe-stepping delicately;
yet (note) always without moving.
He speaks with the throat of buds.
Though the melody of triplets
& iambs repeats, one comes every day
to my wall and sings the tree
where its notes are written.
Tipsy, hopeless, carefree.

The Crow

A dead crow
lay stiffened in a grassy field,
nose-down like a shattered bomber.
Flies changed rings
on its dusty coal-black feathers,
but they fled when I hunkered down.
Curious
how still, how empty of content
was that folded companion, whom
I may have seen any number of times
flapping staidly ahead in carbon silk.

The wind stirred
in its responsive ailerons
and drew a slightly greenish tinge.
The skull stayed
closed on the blunted dagger bill
which a crow's egg chooses to dream.
Was there no
guilty joy when this dawn-raider
stole unhatched chicks and cracked their eggs?
That iron relish, that taste for skewering
eyes, is now referred to the eggs of flies.

Who would wear
this monomaniac's plumage
if he weren't a crow, a blackshirt?
Selection
'makes not up on these conditions.'
My fault that crows exaggerate
the shameless,
mimicking the deplored ego
with jaunty critic's charisma.
This crow dreamed a Viking banner, a beached
longboat, a carved church-pew black as toffee.

Its gaunt beak
won't open to admit a thing—
neither to express the reason
such stillness
disturbs (as though doll's-wood should take root),
nor why the bird fell—here—why this
borderless,
marauding executioner,
a flier of inglorious
missions, called out cast-iron notes in four circles,
these the rusty scissors it used to ply.

The Courting of the Peacock

She sits demurely ignorant,
impassive to his gaudy finery.

In each adjoining kernel
of the fan — FLARED —
Eager Emerald Eyes distend
towards her, geared to hypnotise.

Blue lake, purple, turquoise,
cobalt and viridian,
displaying all his secrets,
conjuring his tail-fan
in a static ecstasy
the peacock bends again,
shifts on his feet
whose petty dancing minces the soil,
and with a brief regular
flurry of vibrated quills
        shudders,
drawing by this breathy fluster
dry fire to enamel glaze.

Though he shakes his rattles
half a dozen times
she inattentively attends,
preening on a log.

I think she notices after all.

Girl on an Outing

The grain of the days is this,
my walled-in feeling. A can
tilted to slake geranium rock:
fingertips gored to smell a rose.

These are your artist's colours:
the walls travel with me even
to Poole, to the sea's wind-surf mobiles.

My snapshots are of birds' wings,
of people crossing the bridge
of red lacquer, of clouds in the bus,
your couples' white curls on seat-tops.

Your heads grow close together,
married like olive-trees: mine,
my dream is an amateur play.

Bulky Cyrano woos pale
student Roxane: wisteria's
green shade makes him a nightingale.
For you to keep is the impression

Of brave thinness, of facing
the test: no one speaks to me.
For whom have I bought these flowers?

I don't dress my feelings
as you do; somewhere else I sit
in bed, obscure as mice in corn-stalks,
hearing the gnats' crybaby moan.

After You've Gone

The candle ribbon smokes
white script in darkness:
shreds and shivers, scented spirals
laddering an iris sky.

Bird-haunted woodland
fold on fold, wheeling in flight,
sends to an elm in Tübingen
one last fanatic thrush.

From sound-box throats calling
back, other waves unravel
the distant miles of road,
owl syrinx and steeple crow

Heard in vaulted corners
of prayer, like a post-horn
probing graves, a challenge
to dead, sleepy eyes that stare.

Tomorrow, equinox will aim
a glassy Sun at prunus
blossom, like the smash of spray
along breakwater walls.

Pegasus

The stables are empty. Very high,
through fingers held against the blue,
something moves, a silver snip.

Calmly squeezing tunnels of vapour,
the white haunches shudder,
seal-smooth, and push thinnest airwaves.

Shoes with buckles pace to the door
again; clatter involuntary hoofs
where swallows once messed the sills.

But no one can cling to his back,
no rider; each blown off by wing-beats
crawls on this dungeon straw,

Watched by the long-lashed eyes of nags;
but he, legs tucked, a toy-soldier's horse,
wins even higher altitudes.

The stalls have that horse-bum smell,
which the lads forking barrows
of manure breathe in and hire out.

Their art is comb-and-paper
music, suspicious of the shoes
whose stiff ears twitch, vulnerable

Every mile of the road; every breath
that jets in a colder air miming
for the sidewinder that purer trail.

Taking a Message

The bird in a paintbox unwraps
its Chinese scroll of mountains.

Crispy fog-patches float
past crags and cones, blue-tinged,

Opening and closing like a fan
on the rider's staircase climb,

Through rocks and pine-clouds,
high up, to a hermit's cell.

Still the bird's thumbs rustle
silk. The rider jumps down.

His Kurdish boots touch moss
on the threshold; but will his news

Press a spring in the turrets
and minarets of flowers?

As the hermit reads,
unexpected tears crumple his skin.

Song twines his grief smaller, still
smaller, an echo the cave receives.

Nearly Caught

I see way down to other faces there,
off-stage in the smallest room.
Piqued, red-rimmed in the mirror,
with flaked skin and puffy eyes,
old-young, and stranger faces,
ones I didn't ask to see.

Way back to the rounded
not the faded face: pertly
a freckled boy waylays me
with a reproaching dream,
as he peers up from the well-bed
to ask me the way home.

Water sprinkles cold benediction
from a blistered, wheezing pipe.
I lower my eyes. It takes more than
soap between the acts, more than
recognition, vain a million times,
to feel a way back to your face.

That lives on without you:
which proves to have been justified,
like a map to islands sunk
beneath the sea, cutaneous terrains
drawn by gravings of stress,
eye-caverns and brow-ridges.

They hide in glassy silver drops,
the ghostly crowds, waiting
to catch your hand unawares
as it slips the soap. They jump
back from this leaf-scattered pane,
which opens like a cellar door.

To Change by Eating

I write to Goethe
every evening 'nature transforms'.
Yes: he is good enough to reply.
Today the thrush is Michelangelo,
he writes,
knocking a mucilaginous slave out
with his chisel in a private shade,
the garden's breeze-stirred mortuary.
Tap, tap,
the Aztec stone
turns a shell into a drum.
You didn't know then,
(the great man says in passing)
that your thrush-song from a treetop
at dusk is how snails sound?
The snail's
slow trombone becomes
a rhapsody by the thrush,
and that becomes a poet's inspiration.
Hence, all snails are sonnets.

Sir Orfeo

Could I live on such fruits?
The Lion, though famished,
does not eat without dignity.
I will pass them by, shoots
of bole fungus, the squished
havana parasols, city
of toadstools on birch roots;
all except this one, dished
up without smooth-gloved enmity
that makes duck taste of boots.
For dessert no anguished
confection, no cute chef's pretty
chef d'oeuvre of egg; this suits
just as well, strawberry fished
from close leaves, sucked without witty
music. Kings may eat roots,
hips, haws, nuts, who've languished
at court, and find brambles pity
them, when the huntsman hoots
in woodland they're banished
to, clawed by lost love's probity.

NOTE: 'Sir Orfeo', the story of Orpheus and Eurydice, appears to have been translated into South-Western English about 1325-1350.

The Emperor's Rose-Petal Dig

What are they like, the dead days,
all the days gone, packed mille-feuille
together, the moments, childhood
seen again, granted the axe to cut?

Granted review, if our lives
weren't rose's crockery, weren't
moments which forget their decision
to last, stuffed like rose-petals now

In the deadwood rubbish-dump
layered with wet-buckled leaves.
My ghost the inheritor then.
The inventor of these moments

Lost to research, outside the dig,
looks at my life. Does it see
an old toolshed with oak flowers
in dust, & reefed cobwebs in the close air?

Directories of the days,
my love in three volumes, stuck
fast with the glue of time's pressure.
Who knows if my body wore this mask,

Pledged before it left the tribe
of childhood not to recognise
the armfuls of its own joys?
Tiberius calls for his skull again,

And wakes, shocked out of the earth,
the sun a cloudy island of flame,
and hears the bark on his skin
wrenched whole from his cork-oak side.

Kennedy's Revised Latin Primer

The green primer with its close-packed leaves,
quick—take to the boats—escape.

The instruments of verbs are safe now,
safer than the passive voice, amáris,
thou art or thou art being loved.

How beautiful—quam pulcher! How far—
quam longe? Year, boy, master, war.
Iamdiu—long since; the fruit
ripens in clusters now, green then.

I have become is represented, sum—I am.
Ubinam gentium sumus—where in the world
are we? Fáre—speak thou! Adolévi—
I grew up. I see the Perfect is just that.
Amávi—I loved; and the Imperfect,
amábas—you were loving, or you loved.

Entertaining Caesar

(Puteoli: 19th December 45 B.C.)

Not liking to refuse his plan
that we should meet again
lest he read my absence as fear,
or 'resistance to the trend
of events', I let him come.

Scholars' respect apart, our friendship
—from times past—I'd never get back
into it, I thought,
any more than a tight robe, but,
his presence thawed the frost

Like the sun on the roofs that morning,
and despite the guards that Cassius
Barba lent me—making the grounds
look like the dictator's
camp—all was friendly.

Still, it was my feeling he came
to test me: about new
vacillations; old decisions;
prompted perhaps by henchmen
who feared my veto on them ...

Or simply from curiosity:
sure in my own mind his private
opinion belittled my past
handling of power and
discounted my 'threat' now.

Threat? — We had three rooms
full of dining retainers and slaves.
Had it not been a slight
to friendship, you could say we leant
over backwards to make him God.

He seemed meaner than before:
one knew he could obligate
bullies like Antony.
His reserve — we discussed only
literary things — was awesome.

For he couldn't quite hide the fact
—despite his walk on the shore, his
bath, his emetic pills —
that he had billeted himself on
me, a friend of Rome,

As if to show his marked contempt
for the freedom he had
ended with gifts, of conquests
arming his greater Empire to crush
those who would kill him.

Arming against Rome,
he had need of guards: for it was
by the stink of power
that the Liberators found him
when the people had no champion.

I was relieved to see him go,
for I had dined with a dead man.

(Cicero himself was murdered one year and nine months later, under proscription by the party of Antony and Octavian.)

Rue Point

Winter's here again.
Is it at all surprising I go back
in my mind to summer days?

I'm going down that winding road
again to Rue Point, past hedgerows
crowded with searing gorse.

The coastline glitters still
and curves into sunlight,
forcing one to shield one's eyes.

Nearby, a coast-guard's hut
faces to sea in blinding heat,
where freighters slide by watery stages.

Fine sand blows under the door.
A dried strop of seaweed on the bench
whiffs of some monster storm.

The sea eats into the land here,
ebb and flow rinse the pebbles
clicking under salty suds.

High in the blue, ice
scarves of alto-cirrus stretch
and fray, long silken miles.

Cold Snap

The boards have aged
overnight in the garden.
Frost, silver as old man's stubble,
beards them with starry hairs.

The clench of glass teeth
stretches when sun hits the oak.
The whole jigsaw breaks,
and trickles bronze leaves earthwards.

A tangle of iris blades
nods in the wind; they are like
Spanish swords, bent in two,
their steel chased with grave designs.

I hug my ribs, and squat
to touch the concrete soil.
I accept its promptings; let
the leaves, white sandpaper,

Rub on my mind, and
watch still how red apples hang
above sugared grass;
ice threaded on woollen webs.

The moon has taken a vow
of silence, its frosted lens
equal as to whether dung or
diamond fills my Trappist mouth.

Anniversaries

This greening wood in the mind,
with one tree singing to another —
who hacked the bark, do you think?
Was it my hand, clean now
and pianistic, my hand that forgot
where to go in at the oak?

The pop-up birds, married, in love,
come and go from blackthorn windows
streaming stars of lace,
yet I misapprehend their instructions.
I am the thought that walls them out.
Their free hedge-hop trajectories,
their blue fans of magpie ink,
wrens swimming the air, crows space-walking
from a tree, are echoes crossing here.

The box of mind, one side acrylic
and the other metal, tightly shuts.
I let in cold thoughts; flakes
of snow, plum blossom that melts
in sunny intervals of sky.

Tulip Folio

Drawn with the finest pencil
our buds are not so green as those,
birch chandeliers, which sparkle
and stream, facing the sun.

Is it blunt, an art that scrapes
the fretsaw of green instruments
of hazel; out of tune, say,
with their catkin celeste?

Or do I copy sediments
of slate-dark clouds, only to make
chestnut leaves hanging like bats
fresher green in every rib and vein?

If I cut, what will the colour be;
furled scarlet like a tulip,
sap white as the juice of trees,
or beaten blue, aquamarine?

I note this music, anyway;
the shudder as a crow's black bar
of shadow strobes across the wood,
under the faded moon.

Painting in the Rain

I inscribe 'grieving', black as rainy script
on this cool wall of pulp,
where it dates a kilroy truth.

Sun lightens the mist of rain,
tufty green fills the valley with trees;
headlamps blaze up on the hill.

Even in hazel lanes the anxious me
comes on behind, unimpressed by beauty;
hard-hearted, it turns a blind eye.

The blue iron cloud is a suspension-bridge.
The brush lets go streamers of rain,
white on a china surface.

Glass

The tree in a drop, snaking down
the window-pane, drags silver.
Branches folded and bending,
each compressed, with nervures
like a wing, free to expand, fall
on microfilm inside a vase of rain.

The tiny image of a man,
likewise compressed, crouches
in a drop, packed tight as a bud,
his teensy face hatched with lines
from a Chinese brush dipped in gum.

On the convexity both travel,
both hesitate together.
Both peer in the oaken mirror,
their see-through net of veins
showing like a mapped-out leaf
drawn in the trickling glass.

The iron grip, the blue devices,
give after this drop one other.

Ariel

I name this vapour that forms
in the trees a shape that blows buds
like green glass on sycamore rods.
It makes gold crucibles of corms.

It wants a clear mirror — the heart.
Grey pelmets, clouds ruched with white
dazzle, it is they show the streaks
engraved on glass, a rain of darts.

Bowling along in the car,
I see branch after branch release
its petal galaxy, each prunus
nebula a shell of stars.

With his tail down a blackbird sings
in secret characters, his perch
the catalpa, outlined in a dusk
of blue darkness such as rain brings.

Circles on water — each bud,
each twig, has its drop, each drop
a setting sun. Bird's notes
vibrate on overflowing mud.

Portrait of a Pear

                The wasps in her skull
                make her a hollow idol,
a green obelisk in the autumn grass.
                She has French perfume,
that clings to my skin; in her bruise's groove
                she has tears of alcohol,
her red flush is like a gasp of impasse,
                her medicinal bloom
dulled like frost on dawn roofs.
She is a Big Bather in luncheon grass,
                her foot stamps the orchard.
She is Madame, the artist's wife, who improves
                with age; whose curves tortured
an aesthete with desire; but now she's gross,
a portly amphora of juice propped in the grass,
                a broken jug I kiss,
                    like waves washing a shell,
a looted wreck on an autumn atoll.

Damsons

Damsons are like insults.
Hard as hornblende
even when ripe, hard to swallow.
A scattering of blue stones,
veiled like mysterious planets
with slight bands of clouds
stretched like tissue on their skin,
they lie staining the pavement.
And a bird shouts in the bracken,
its crepitant fronds
a taste coming into my mouth,
a stiff poison set in a trap,
a furred sour gum of green
as inescapable as babies' tears.
This proves the stone of knowledge,
the iron heart at the centre
on which teeth bite in vain:
and all the truth of bitterness
which is an incorruptible fruit,
and answers nothing
to pleas, enquiries, and prayers.

English Discovery

I study the map, its sweet smell
and sour shock, the boss
of its pink and scarlet shield, polished
with my cuff under moonlight
to a smiling wax, gravely enceinte:
the disconnected globe, from blossom
wet in the grass, showing its green
continents, its gold-red walls of fire.

It is as I say the pallor of orchards,
the tissue fruit are wrapped in:
but this sweet smell, tempting my teeth
to open the round volume, and find
a place in its glistening snows,
whose flavour carves out cliffs
sharp as alchy cider juice,
wins back my boyhood, apple years.

All the years are apple years, eaten
by moonlight: but this chomp
in a windfall, its sweet smell
and sour shock, its cordillera of pulp,
reads out a seashore, a silver plane
flying over a coast, a car-ride home,
a gate, a tidal wave of August
trees, curved over grass intensely green.

And this hand—closing on an apple,
pulling down tight-fisted reds
each with a bursting golden rocket
in a crimson sky, climbing still
through leaves up sinewy boles—
must contemplate itself a boy's:
a prisoner in the central cage
whose white pips are eaten round.

West Green Garden

He trusts us not to ruin beds.
The day is hot, writing is bothersome,
the iron gate has an easy latch,
and Adam the gardener leaves point-of-sales
to itself, a table and chair,
and crunches, somewhere off, on the gravel.

He trusts us not to ruin beds
of wine and ice-cream rambler roses, shrubs
with light censers, box-hedges trimmed
by sunshine, arches' foreshortened green;
it is music, after all,
the freedom of gardens, the drowsy air.

I see Adam as humping urns
of marigolds, and meeting us half way.
Meeting? — well, passing through, his flowers
some over, some green like miniature domes;
and he offers to those who try
his urn that smell of sharp-sweet irritant.

Why? One wants to ask all questions
twice — the afternoon's so hot; the beds so
braided with bees; even the fruit's
locked in an iron cage — why the violet
black beetle should trust in the stones,
and not fly, fly, from Adam's paradise?

Night of Stars

Gently the sand cooled beneath our pressing feet
and the stars so long forgotten
dived in warm silence
through the night scented with flowering trees.

An old man shouted at the sky,
his words tumbling down the rotten staircase
from a balcony; our footsteps caught
in the thick draughts of lingering grains.

Nowhere was the darkness more alluring.
Wading into the sea; and underfoot
the stones slid down to fathomless blackness
and the stars dropped melting in our eyes.

The air was cold on coming out
and the reeds, where we slept, were plagued
with biting sand-flies, and a cock crew, hoarsely,
in the hills as the moon broke free.

All through the small hours in the town
a wakened dog barked, barked, irritated
by this sickle overhead, reflected
drinking on the waters indolently lapping.

Sharp, Bright, Dark

       The thorns lecture us
       from slopes of lion hay.
Up to the crest, hardship their theme, susurrus
pulls their tattered wigs of seed awry.
       Their girdles of knives
       group on the hill to shield
the hardness of a sunny wall from the green
missions of basil and thyme, whose yield
measures the day in loud vaults of hives.

       I have those echoing seas
       inside my head. Groves,
always shaping the silence with cicadas;
the earth like pipe-clay, drying its mauves
       and greys, its orange straw;
       the wind turning leaves
of olives, cutting the brightness of that deep
blue. The smoke of twilight slowly grieves
into an empty sky from a black shore.

       Summer's last fling has
       no predicted beauty
for the joyful eye that names this the season
of rhinestone cobwebs. Sniff the fruity
       papers of toadstools,
       smelling of decay. Ask
if your name appears in their books. Watch the bars
tired ants frequent, dark holes in a cask,
as their chalky theatre fades and cools.

The Kaleidoscope

It won't convince the real adults.
They look in the top, the deep
triangular well, turning it round

with superstitious hands,

giving it experimental shakes.
The broken child's telescope,
the tube with a trapped star writhing.

Shake. No magic leaks from the fault.
The blue instrument will sleep
more years dreaming of an eye discerned

far off at the sharp end.

The vanman seizes it by the neck
and lobs it into the skip
where its delicate glass walls break.

The toy slides out on the rubbish-tip
with junk cleared from the red house,
and looks about it with a pure eye.

Shake. The flat pips of foil,

teased by hand to irregular shapes,
regroup and settle, hold tight
to lost diffraction formulae.

The eye-flute with the crystal stops
made good music. You despise
wrongly the first as the puerile.

The first eye saw rare jewels.

The images that light your workshop
come out of just such a tube.
The drab yields the iridescent.

The Argument from Forgotten Corners

Cars back up to this hedge and puff
poisonous plumes on the leaves,
which have no choice but to grow there.
The main road wafts a crisp-bag
onto the tresses of ivy-leaved toadflax,
beneath which is home for some few
second-class insects confined
to a tent-city of mouldy brown leaves.

I collect all unnoticed things.
Wherever an old bed is dumped,
and green shadows come and go
on its striped ticking, wherever
an old blue pump smelling of oil
goes rusty in a by-road shed,
still loyal to discontinued amenities,
I take up the argument.

There's no honesty in razzmatazz.
Who cares if music demands white tie
and tails, champagne and limousines?
The creeper, bearding this deserted house
from top to gutter, knows more
in C minor than buyers rehearsing
postures of proprietorship,
pacing its dusty boards on a Saturday.

I reserve for last the magnificent
scooter, tucked away behind the view,
sunk to the brakes in lisping sand,
going nowhere on a summer dune,
sans wheels, sans paint, sans everything.

All Vagrom Men

A derelict sat in the Tube,
knees drawn with his can, facing the crowd,
thousands hourly mangling in streams
through tunnels where no one thinks aloud.

One among them stopped and stood,
bending to feed coins from her purse
into his lap, where his hand followed hers,
now patting him like a nurse.

On his hair straggly as a Gaul's
with long rat-tails, she planted a kiss.
His eyes turned, watching her back,
his face a dirty brown like liquorice.

Soup Kitchen

Their faces speak like cries
heard from within rock walls.
Their spirits are trapped in a cave,
too deep for clumsy charity to find.

One row drinks. Another waits. A chef
in white holds out a ladle of broth.
To each, helpers hand out buttered bread.
Wheeled urns creak nearer down the line.

A hush steals over the long hall
with its brown paint, its paper chains.
With weary eyes some stare at the table.
The spoons sound like steel rain.

Hunter Gatherer

I stumbled like a dense seeker
painting darkness with his smoky torch,
and fell into the cave.
Black as lamplit eyes,
the live rock flexing bulls.
My hands spoke their forbidden language,
it was *my* skin arrows pierced.

Curious, as to the dead, why
their lipless screams resembled
sexual grins, it was proved to me
how corpse hands, dragging,
gripped the sand.

I feared those wicker baskets
crammed with living dead.
The neat huts row on row.
There *is* evil. These
are its rotten fruit; corpses
piled in their mnemonic rings.

Paris: Winter Night

Small wonder the poets of modern life
feel oppressed by the city. A cab-horse
droops its head against wind keen as a knife.

Scurrying figures vanish into coarse
hallways, as if to escape conversion.
It's all dead matter wheeling round the Bourse.

Absinthe Paris represents aversion —
to the horror of being stuck mid-way
down a shaft resounding with assertions.

Sleet pelts the mussel-black roofs and doorways,
round café lamps where gourmands eat pink roe;
the bridge where beggars stare at rumbling drays.

Two hobnail boots splash in the filthy snow,
dreaming of when they were painted, a day
of Naples blue, the language of swallows.

Apparitions

Van Gogh, Letter W22 to his sister Wilhelmina:
'... I *should like* to paint portraits which would appear after a century to the people living then as apparitions.'

      One seems to be listening to sunlight,
to horse-drawn carriages on avenues way below,
      to thoughts of flight on trains.
The haunted eyes remain unflinching,
      & ask whether things have changed at all?
Artists starving.
      Living on coffee and bread.
A Japanese and shaven cranium.
      The work throws an electric net
round a creature shaped by his acts,
      whose soul is distinct from these torments,
pushing the known image forward
      like a memory,
its seeker the will, not the five senses.
      Piped with blue ribbon,
jacket and waistcoat stand alone, empty
      save for a ghost that lurks inside the bone.
The faces are as many as the acts.

The Sower

Mine the butcher's grip, easing off
the one corner of original vision held,
so tight, the quiver of brush-strokes shakes
like a lover's hand unbuttoning a blouse.

The sun painted in daffodil glaze
quivers lightly as fluid gold,
shivering in a silent centrifuge.
The sower flings at each abyss of clods.

The brush-marks are like sunflower-seeds.
Ankle-plumes of dust drift at his feet.
He eyes my back. Sun gilds his shirt.
We speak Provençal like swallows.

The Asylum at St. Rémy

They sit in a daydream, these
patients in a third-class waiting-room,
signalling, as if to trains,
their strayed lives which don't exist.

In top hat and coat they tease
invisible companions: the boom
of locked doors echoes in brains
so shaken they daren't resist.

The horror that seeks the hearth
of their minds can sometimes be heard

Down there: all day long screaming
and howling till ones heart quietly breaks.
And the cart, with ones things tied
on, sinks in a flooded road.

I don't know if I'm dreaming,
but sometimes vermicular Tersteeg
comes to ask if I have died
and squats nearby like a toad.

'Now see where your incorrectness
has landed you.—New technique!'

To escape his sour intrigue
against me I must paddle the creek
quite slowly at first, and dog
the white star haunting the track.

His name is the sound my clogs make,
clacking round bleak stone-walled murk.

The Dark Side of the Moon

The squeak of an axle hidden
by fields — heard as it jars —
will bring the cart to a midden
lit by a single star.

Not sent for, the beds, the tables
shift, in a decrepit
room; none with a forward label —
one easel excepted.

There are barns in a Brabant town
with pictures for windows;
on attic doors a portrait's frown,
dirt cheap off a barrow.

Silent in a drawer, his many
letters in yellow piles
— to post which might cost last pennies —
travel through time in style.

A stifling garret, an iron bed,
wait for feet on the stairs.
A glass vibrates as thunder sheds
its white electric scare.

Baudelaire's Second Lecture

It was one of those Indian ink days.
The poet spruce and confident
stepped to the rostrum — gripped bombazeen lapels
with hands that worked in funerary style —
and dropped a brick.

Loose language — bawdy words. Necks turned,
bustles like black turkeys swelled in the aisles.
Come, children! His neat hand, to contain
the gabbling exodus, strayed from his cuff.
There on its glacis was a smutty mark.

Hand withdrew. Seats emptied fast.
His lips tasted Cyprus lemon-juice,
tobacco words to chew and spit. Soon,
only one young man sat listening
with a burning, crimson face.

Later in Paris Baudelaire met Catulle Mendès.
The poet was a very different man
from the former dandy, more like a dosser
in a dirty suit, unkempt, no luggage,
with a frightened ill-looking white face.

Mendès offered him a couch for the night.
In the dark he woke and heard the poet
weeping next door, thinking none but himself
awake, the sound as strange as torch-light
probing a cave bearded with stalactites.

Fearing to go in, he let well alone.
It was raining from dish-clout skies,
gas-lamps gleamed on black hoods,
the plane-trees dripped dark drops of fog.
Perhaps he had imagined it — the sound.

High flats do permit such noises.
Old hags and drunks, prowling in the yard
at night, can sound like that,
posing their grief as a siren song.
But the next day Baudelaire was gone.

Kafka in the Cinema

The tree grows rain: the cotton sky (a cone
      of light, where it snows dust idly drifting,
tethered to the wall) fades and loses tone;
      the reels clitter. A Chaplin film can bring
this tight-knit lawyer to tears; appalling
      him — how easy now to love and rebel,
especially if it involves nothing
      more real than the ghost-images of hell.

The tree grows rain every time he's alone
      in the dark auditorium. Listening
to some cheap romance from his armchair throne.
      Look — the bow lips and kohl eyes, fluttering
for a made-good hero, cringe from the sting
      of a wasp jigging above a sweet smell;
and the horned light makes their happy dancing
      more real than the ghost-images of hell.

The tree grows rain. This one is made of stone,
      ashen in the city square whose gales sing
through tram-wires with a creepy, haunting moan
      as he steps out, his black coat billowing
like a sail, tormented by not wishing
      enough to be rescued by an angel;
for the heart keeps its ghetto, the one thing
      more real than the ghost-images of hell.

Kaf-Kaf-Kaf-Kaf-Ka! the spool clacks, breaking
      off the illusion. And light (how to tell
a dog's life) makes your eyes fill with yearning,
      more real than the ghost-images of hell.